SHANG DYNASTY

KS2 HISTORY

ALEX WOOLF

Badger Publishing Limited
Oldmeadow Road,
Hardwick Industrial Estate,
King's Lynn PE30 4JJ
Telephone: 01438 791037

www.badgerlearning.co.uk

2 4 6 8 10 9 7 5 3

The Shang Dynasty ISBN 978-1-78464-068-2

Text: © Alex Woolf 2015
Complete work © Badger Publishing Limited 2015

All rights reserved. No part of this publication may be reproduced, stored in any form or by any means mechanical, electronic, recording or otherwise without the prior permission of the publisher.

The right of Alex Woolf to be identified as author of this work has been asserted by him in accordance with the Copyright, Designs and Patents Act 1988.

Publisher: Susan Ross
Project editor: Paul Rockett
Designer: Jo Digby Designs

Picture credits:
The Art Archive/Beijing Institute of Archaeology/Granger Collection 17; © Art Directors & TRIP/Alamy 18, 23; © Asian Art & Archaeology, Inc./CORBIS 25, 30; King Wen of Zhou/British Library, London, UK/© British Library Board. All Rights Reserved/Bridgeman Images 28; The British Museum 11; © Burstein Collection/CORBIS 24; © China Images/Alamy 7, 30; © B Christopher/Alamy 15; akg-images/De Agostini Picture Lib. 13; © Lowell Georgia/Corbis 29; © LOOK Die Bildagentur der Fotografen GmbH/Alamy 27; © STRINGER/CHINA/Reuters/Corbis 19; CC. Wikimedia Commons cover, 4, 6, 8, 9, 12, 14, 16, 21, 22, 26; woaiss/Shutterstock 10.

Attempts to contact all copyright holders have been made.
If any omitted would care to contact Badger Learning, we will be happy to make appropriate arrangements

THE SHANG DYNASTY

Contents

1. WHO WERE THE SHANG? 5
2. SHANG SOCIETY 6
3. ARTS AND CRAFTS 12
4. SCIENCE AND WRITING 18
5. RELIGION 24
6. THE END OF THE SHANG 28
QUESTIONS 31
INDEX 32

Badger LEARNING

Vocabulary

Do you know these words? Look them up in a dictionary and then see how they are used in the book.

bartered

inscriptions

irrigate

lacquer

merchants

nomadic

predictions

rituals

1. Who were the Shang?

The Shang were a dynasty of kings who ruled over part of northern China from about 1600 to 1046 BCE.

The Shang people were mainly farmers, but were also skilled workers in bronze, bone, jade, stone and ceramics. They developed a calendar and also China's first writing system.

2. SHANG SOCIETY

The king was the most powerful person in Shang society. Beneath him were the nobles, followed by the priests, soldiers, craftspeople, merchants, farmers and slaves.

The king had a team of officials to help him rule. They may have been members of his family. The officials organised the collection of taxes from the farmers.

King Tang of Shang, the first king of the Shang dynasty

Burials

We know how important people were from the way they were buried. Kings and nobles had large tombs filled with beautiful objects. The poorest people were buried in small pits in the ground.

HISTORY HIGHLIGHT!

Hundreds of slaves were buried alive in the royal tomb along with the dead king.

The royal tomb of Queen Fu Hao, who died in 1200 BCE

War

The Shang kings often fought wars with neighbouring peoples. Nobles would provide the kings with soldiers. The kings and nobles led their troops into battle.

Shang soldiers wore armour of bamboo and cloth. They fought with bronze swords, spears, pole-axes, dagger-axes and bows. They rode horse-drawn chariots.

Some weapons had decorative designs, like this battle-axe with a human face.

Oracle bones

Shang kings used 'oracle bones' to make predictions about the future. A scribe would carve a question into a bone, such as 'Will we win the battle?'

A hot metal rod would then be inserted into the bone until it cracked. The king or a priest would interpret the cracks to work out the answer.

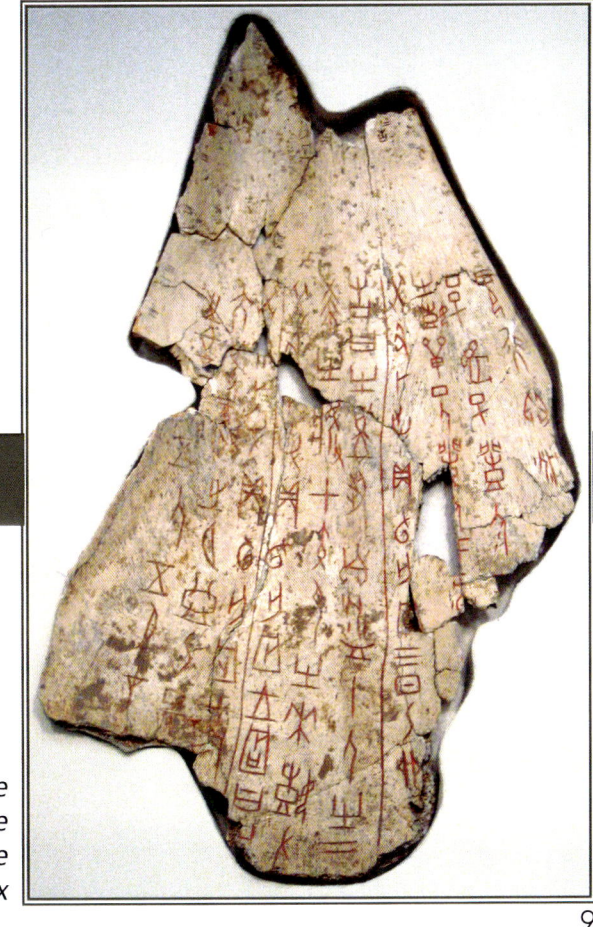

Oracle bone carving on the shoulder blade of an ox

Farming

The Shang lived in the fertile Yellow River valley. They farmed millet, wheat, rice and barley.
They built a system of canals and dams to irrigate their lands and prevent flooding.

Shang farmers used water buffalo to pull ploughs. They raised pigs, sheep and chickens. They also farmed silkworms for making luxury silk garments.

Many farmers in China still use water buffalos to pull ploughs.

Transport and trade

Kings and nobles travelled by chariot, but most people went on foot. Oxen were used to transport heavy goods.

All Shang cities were on a river, and boats and rafts carried cargo to the cities.

Shang merchants traded goods at city markets. They bartered, or used cowrie shells for money.

Shang dynasty cowrie shells

3. ARTS AND CRAFTS

The Shang were skilled craftworkers. They created fine objects out of many different materials, including:
- bronze
- jade
- ceramic
- turquoise
- ivory
- stone
- bone
- tortoise shell

They painted with inks on silk, and coated wood, metal and bamboo objects with lacquer to give them a beautiful finish.

Plaque from 15th–13th century BCE, made of bronze and turquoise

Bronze making

The Shang were masters of the art of bronze making. They cast bronze in ceramic moulds to make tools, weapons, containers, musical instruments and chariot fittings.

Royal tombs contained hundreds of small bronze objects, including knives, mirrors, bells, animal statues and even hairpins.

Bronze elephant drinking vessel from 11th century BCE

Ritual bronze vessels

The Shang kings required large numbers of bronze vessels for religious ceremonies. These were produced in royal workshops.

The vessels were inscribed with patterns resembling animal faces, including tigers, snakes, dragons and owls. Some vessels had long feet so that a fire could be lit beneath to cook the food inside.

Bronze vessel, from around 11th century BCE

Musical instruments

Improvements in bronze casting techniques enabled the Shang to produce musical instruments out of bronze, as well as wood, stone and ceramic.

They made bronze cymbals, drums, gongs and bells. They also made chime stones and xuns (egg-shaped ceramic wind instruments).

Bronze bell, 12th century BCE

Ceramics

Shang craftspeople also produced grey or white pottery vessels decorated with patterns identical to those found on bronze vessels.

Some of their pots were covered with a thin, yellow-green glaze – the first examples of glazed pottery in China.

HISTORY HIGHLIGHT!

The tomb of Fu Hao, wife of King Wu-ting, contained 468 works of bronze and 775 pieces of jade.

Jade

Jade was highly prized by the Shang. The number of jade objects a person owned was a sign of their status. Carvings were often used in offerings to the gods and in royal ceremonies.

Shang craftspeople carved jade into animal shapes. Discs of jade were intricately carved with images of dragons, fish, tigers, birds and ox-like creatures, as well as geometric patterns.

Bird pendent made of jade, 1300–1030 BCE

4. SCIENCE AND WRITING

The Shang needed a way of measuring the seasons so that they would know when to plant and harvest crops and when to perform religious ceremonies.

Calendar

They developed a calendar with a 360-day year made up of 12 months of 30 days each. The year was also subdivided into ten-day weeks.

Chinese zodiac characters originate from the early Chinese calendars

The calendar was based on the cycles of the Moon and the Sun. Because the two cycles don't match up, a short extra month was added every few years to keep them in step.

To this day, the Chinese calendar is based on the cycles of the Moon and Sun. This is why Chinese New Year falls on a different date each year.

Mathematics

To calculate the calendar, the Shang needed some mathematics. Evidence from oracle bones suggests they:

- could count up to thirty thousand
- could distinguish between odd and even numbers
- developed a decimal system.

Astronomy

The Shang observed the movements of the Sun, Moon and stars in order to create their calendar. They calculated the solar year as 365¼ days.

Inscriptions have been found on animal bones and tortoise shells recording some of their observations. These include records of solar and lunar eclipses.

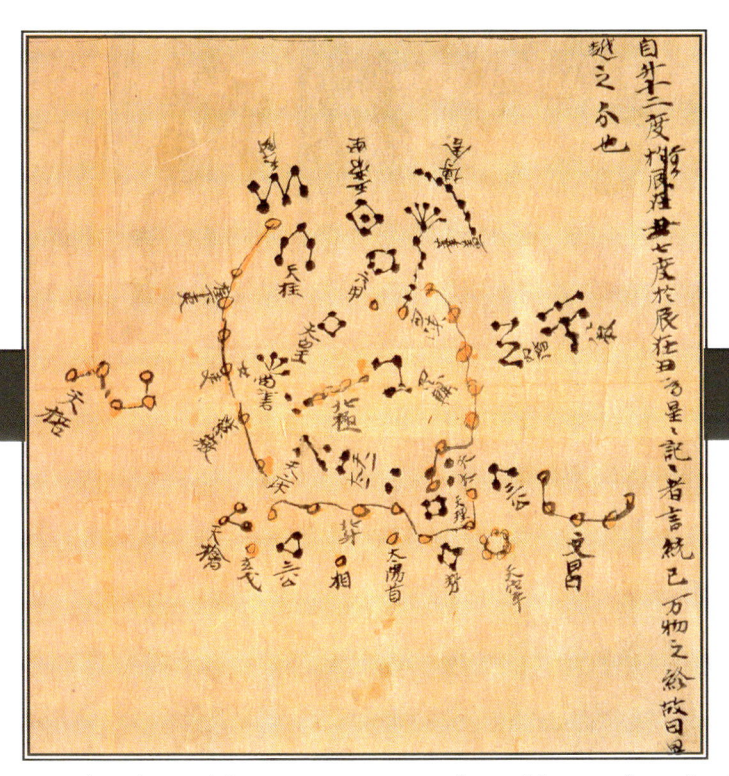

Fascination with astronomy continued long after the Shang Dynasty. This Chinese map of the stars is from 700 CE.

Writing

The Shang developed a system of writing consisting of about 5,000 characters. Each character is made of two parts – the first giving its meaning, the second its pronunciation.

Scribes usually wrote on thin bamboo strips. For this reason, characters were usually written vertically. Later, scribes wrote on rice paper and silk.

None of the bamboo, paper and silk writings have lasted. The earliest examples of Chinese writing have been found on Shang oracle bones, tortoise and turtle shells and bronze vessels.

HISTORY HIGHLIGHT!

Modern Chinese writing developed out of the system first created by the Shang 3,500 years ago.

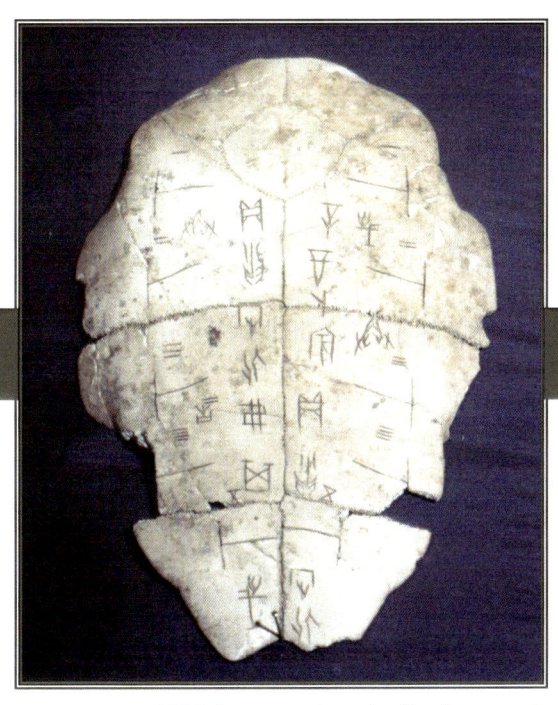

Writing on the shell of a turtle

5. RELIGION

The Shang believed in many gods. They worshipped and made sacrifices to them to keep them happy.

They also worshipped their ancestors, who they believed lived in the spirit world.

Wine-pouring vessel used for rituals

Shang Ti

Shang Ti, the 'lord on high', was the most important god.

He was responsible for natural forces like the wind and rain. He could cause disasters such as flood, drought and sickness and could control the outcome of battles.

It was therefore very important to ensure that Shang Ti was happy. People did this through rituals and prayers, making offerings and sometimes even human sacrifices.

The faces on this ceremonial cooking vessel are thought to be those of gods or spirits.

Other gods

The people also prayed to natural gods like the Earth, the Yellow River, Mount Song and the Sun. Dead kings were turned into gods and given the title of *Di*.

HISTORY HIGHLIGHT!

When a king died, humans and dogs would be sacrificed to help the king's spirit in the afterlife.

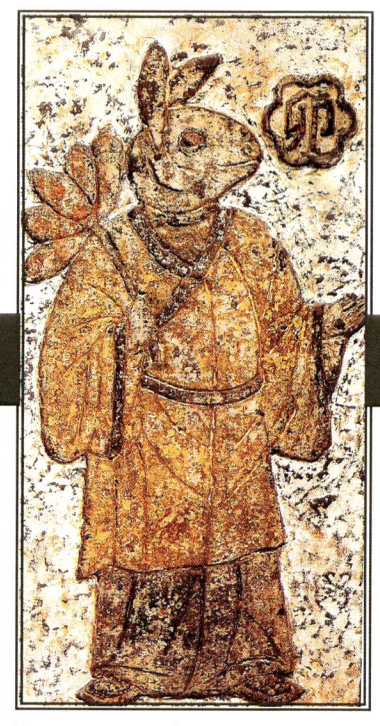

Later painting, showing guardian spirits of Day and Night

Ancestor worship

The Shang believed that the spirits of their ancestors visited Shang Ti and received instructions from him.

They prayed to their ancestors for guidance and protection. They made offerings of food and wine, which they placed in bronze vessels.

In China today, people still pray and make offerings to their ancestors

6. THE END OF THE SHANG

Towards the end of the Shang period, the dynasty was weakened by frequent wars with nomadic tribes and rival kingdoms in China.

The last Shang king was Shang Zhou. According to tradition, he was a cruel man who led a life of luxury and tortured and imprisoned many of his people.

King Wen, leader of the Zhou people, an enemy kingdom

Defeat

Around 1046 BCE, Shang Zhou was defeated by an army of a rival clan at the Battle of Muye. Confusingly, the name of this clan was also Zhou.

This brought an end to the Shang dynasty and marked the beginning of the Zhou dynasty, which ruled China for the next 800 years.

HISTORY HIGHLIGHT!
After his defeat, Shang Zhou gathered his treasures around him, set fire to his palace and committed suicide.

Although the Shang army had more soldiers, the Zhou were better trained and had war chariots, like these, found buried with their horses.

Legacy of the Shang

The Shang developed the earliest writing system in China. The period also witnessed important advances in bronze and pottery making.

However, perhaps the most lasting legacy of the Shang was that they showed how it was possible to create a civilised state with a powerful king. This provided a model for future Chinese dynasties.

Shang bronze sculpture of a tiger

Monument to the Shang Dynasty, on the site of its capital city

QUESTIONS

Why did Shang kings use oracle bones? *(page 9)*

Which river flowed through the lands controlled by the Shang? *(page 10)*

What did the Shang use for money? *(page 11)*

Name some of the musical instruments the Shang made. *(page 15)*

How long was a week in the Shang calendar? *(page 18)*

Why were Chinese characters written vertically? *(page 22)*

Who was the last king of the Shang? *(page 28)*

INDEX

ancestor worship 24, 27
astronomy 21

bone 5, 9, 12, 21
bronze 5, 8, 12, 13, 14, 15, 16, 30
bronze vessels 14, 23, 27

calendar 5, 18-19, 20, 21
ceramics 5, 12, 15, 16, 30
chariots 8, 11, 13, 29
craftworkers 6, 12, 16, 17

farming 5, 6, 10, 18

gods 17, 24, 25, 26

jade 5, 12, 16, 17

kings 5, 6, 7, 8, 11, 14, 26, 28, 29, 30

mathematics 20
merchants 6, 11
musical instruments 13, 15

nobles 6, 7, 8, 11

oracle bones 9, 20, 23

priests 6, 9

religion 14, 17, 18, 24-27

sacrifice 24, 25, 26
scribes 9, 22
Shang Ti 25, 27
Shang Zhou 28-29
silk 10, 12, 22
slaves 6, 7
soldiers 6, 8, 29

taxes 6
tombs 7 13, 16
trade 11
transport 11

war 8, 28, 29
weapons 8, 13
writing 5, 9, 22-23, 30

Zhou dynasty 29